Butterfly or Moth

Which Is Which?

By Tamra B. Orr

21st Century **Junior** Library

Published in the United States of America by
Cherry Lake Publishing
Ann Arbor, Michigan
www.cherrylakepublishing.com

Reading Adviser: Marla Conn, MS, Ed., Literacy specialist, Read-Ability, Inc.
Content Adviser: Susan Heinrichs Gray

Photo Credits: ©Marcia Straub/Shutterstock, cover (left); ©Tony Campbell/Shutterstock, cover (right); ©DuyMy/Shutterstock, 4; ©Felicia Dawn Hamberg/Shutterstock, 6; ©Pankaj Ghare/Shutterstock, 8; ©SanderMeertinsPhotography/Shutterstock, 10; ©Dragona99/Shutterstock, 12; Cocos.Bounty/Shutterstock, 14; ©Lars Espeter Photography/Shutterstock, 16; ©rimom/Shutterstock, 18; ©Ilia Ustyantsev/flickr, 20

Library of Congress Cataloging-in-Publication Data

Names: Orr, Tamra, author.
Title: Butterfly or moth / Tamra B. Orr.
Description: Ann Arbor : Cherry Lake Publishing, [2019] | Series: Which is which? | Includes bibliographical references and index. | Audience: K to Grade 3.
Identifiers: LCCN 2019006011 | ISBN 9781534147386 (hardcover) | ISBN 9781534150249 (paperback) | ISBN 9781534148819 (pdf) | ISBN 9781534151673 (hosted ebook)
Subjects: LCSH: Butterflies—Juvenile literature. | Moths—Juvenile literature.
Classification: LCC QL544.2 .O77 2019 | DDC 595.78/9—dc23
LC record available at https://lccn.loc.gov/2019006011

Cherry Lake Publishing would like to acknowledge the work of the Partnership for 21st Century Skills. Please visit *www.p21.org* for more information.

Printed in the United States of America
Corporate Graphics

CONTENTS

5 Insect Scales

9 Clubs or Feathers?

13 Wonderful Wings

17 Cocoon and Chrysalis

22 Glossary

23 Find Out More

24 Index

24 About the Author

Butterflies and moths can "hear" sounds through their wings.

Insect Scales

Did you see that? Something small and colorful just flew by. It was too big to be a bee. It was too small to be a bird. What was it? Take a closer look. It has four wings, six legs, and two **antennae**. Is it a moth or a butterfly? Many people often confuse one for the other. Look closer. Can you tell which is which?

Moths and butterflies have a lot in common. Both are known as *lepidoptera*, which means "scaly-winged." This is because their wings

Some moths don't eat. They live only for a week after emerging from their cocoon.

are covered in tiny scales like hair. These scales fall off or are shed throughout their lives.

Moths and butterflies both start their lives as eggs. Next, they develop into hungry caterpillars. They snack on the sweet **nectar** found in flowers. They also sip drops of water left on leaves and petals after a rain. They are alike in so many ways, but different in just as many.

Look!

A number of moths fool people into thinking they are butterflies. Unlike typical moths, these moths have brightly colored wings and fly during the day. Peru's green-banded *Urania* is one of them. This moth shares many characteristics of butterflies. So do moth **species** found in Indonesia and Australia.

Butterflies use their feet to "taste!"

Clubs or Feathers?

Moths and butterflies start out looking a lot alike. But they change quite a bit as they grow. Butterflies tend to have long, thin bodies without any hair on them. A moth's body is thicker and usually fuzzy with hair. Butterflies tend to be bigger than moths.

Butterflies and moths use their antennae the same way. Both insects use them to guide them when they fly. The insects also use them like noses! The antennae are covered in tiny hairs. Each hair helps the

Many moths look like things they aren't—from hornets to owl eyes to even bird poop!

insects to smell other moths and butterflies nearby. As they fly, the antennae tend to be held out and up.

Though the use is the same, the antennae look different in both insects. Butterflies have long antennae with a club or knob shape at the end. Most moths have slender antennae that end in a point. Some have feathery antennae, much like combs.

Make a Guess!

Moths and butterflies have different forelegs, or front legs. The front legs of a moth are larger than a butterfly's. Some butterflies have forelegs that are really small. It might even look like the insect has only four legs! How would this change the way the insects fly and land?

Butterflies can't fly if the temperature is less than 85 degrees Fahrenheit (29 degrees Celsius).

Wonderful Wings

What's a quick way to tell the difference between a moth and a butterfly? Look at their wings. A butterfly's wings are usually brighter and more colorful than a moth's. A butterfly often has spots of orange, blue, purple, or red. Moths tend to be shades of white, brown, and gray.

The way each insect rests its wings also sets the two apart. Butterflies fold their wings together above their bodies when they land. This means you can see the undersides

The smallest moth measures just 0.05 inches (1.3 millimeters). The largest moth measures 12 inches (30 centimeters) from wingtip to wingtip!

of their wings. Moths, however, spread their wings out when they rest.

The way they fly is also different. Moths have a **frenulum**. This is a part of their body that connects the front wings to the back wings. When they fly, the wings move together. A butterfly's wings overlap. They aren't connected. In flight, a butterfly's front wings push the back wings down when its wings flap down.

Think!

Butterflies usually fly and feed during the day. Moths usually fly and feed at night. Why do you think this is? Use the internet and your library to study this topic further.

Skipper butterflies can fly faster than a horse's gallop! But on average, butterflies fly 5 to 12 miles (8 to 19 kilometers) per hour.

Cocoon and Chrysalis

It is difficult to tell a moth and a butterfly apart when they are caterpillars. But they will turn from a long, worm-like shape to a winged one. Look at where they each go when it is time to change. Then it is clear which one is which.

Moth and butterfly caterpillars turn into a soupy mush once inside their cocoon or chrysalis.

Both insects make a protective shell in order to change into their last form. A butterfly makes a **chrysalis** and a moth makes a cocoon. A butterfly's chrysalis is hard and smooth. A moth's cocoon is usually covered in silk that the caterpillar has spun. Often it is covered in leaves. This makes it harder for **predators** to see in. Both insects are in their coverings for 5 to 21 days before hatching. How long

There are some butterflies and moths, like this vampire moth, that drink the blood of animals!

moths and butterflies live depends on many **factors**. Most only live a few weeks or less.

Watch for winged creatures flying by. Then look closely. See if you can figure out if it is a butterfly or a moth.

Ask Questions!

The painted lady butterfly is one of the longest-living butterflies. It can live up to an entire year. What factors do you think might control how long a butterfly or moth lives?

GLOSSARY

antennae (an-TEN-ee) long feelers on the heads of insects

chrysalis (KRIS-uh-lis) the hard outer case that protects a caterpillar when transforming

factors (FAK-turz) things that help produce a result

frenulum (FREN-yoo-lum) a part on the body of a moth that attaches its front and back wings

nectar (NEK-tur) the sweet liquid produced by flowering plants

predators (PRED-uh-turz) animals that live by hunting other animals for food

species (SPEE-sheez) a group of animals that are similar and can produce young animals

FIND OUT MORE

BOOKS

Butterflies and Moths: Explore Nature with Fun Facts and Activities. New York, NY: DK Publishing, 2018.

Claybourne, Anna. *Insects in 30 Seconds: 30 Incredible Topics for Bug Boffins Explained in Half a Minute.* UK: Ivy Kids, 2015.

Marsh, Sarah Glenn. *The Bug Girl: Maria Merian's Scientific Vision.* Chicago, IL: Albert Whitman and Company, 2019.

Rustad, Martha. *Magnificent Moths.* North Mankato, MN: Capstone Press, 2017.

WEBSITES

Easy Science for Kids—Butterflies and Moths

https://easyscienceforkids.com/all-about-butterflies-and-moths
Read more about the differences and similarities between these fascinating winged insects.

YouTube—Butterfly or Moth?

https://www.youtube.com/watch?v=iblveeTDkXQ
Watch an informative video about moths and butterflies.

INDEX

A

antennae, 5, 9, 11

B

butterflies
- antennae, 11
- chrysalis, 19
- feet, 8
- flying, 12, 15, 16
- legs, 11
- life span, 21
- size, 9
- what they look like, 9
- wings, 13, 15

C

caterpillars, 7, 17, 18, 19
chrysalis, 18, 19
cocoon, 6, 18, 19
colors, 7, 13

E

eating, 6, 7, 20
eggs, 7

F

feet, 8
flying, 9, 11, 12, 15, 16

H

hair, 9, 11
hatching, 19

L

legs, 5, 11
lepidoptera, 5
life span, 21

M

moths
- antennae, 11
- cocoons, 19
- eating, 6
- flying, 15
- legs, 11
- size, 14
- what they look like, 9, 10
- wings, 13, 15

N

nectar, 7

S

scales, 7
sounds, 4

T

tasting, 8

W

wings, 4, 5, 7, 13, 15

ABOUT THE AUTHOR

Tamra Orr is the author of hundreds of books for readers of all ages. She graduated from Ball State University, but moved with her husband and four children to Oregon in 2001. She is a full-time author, and when she isn't researching and writing, she writes letters to friends all over the world. Orr enjoys life in a suburb of Portland, where she often spots butterflies and moths and always takes a moment to appreciate them.